Preface - Embracing Grace and Dignity in Employee Termination

In the complex and often challenging world of business, the art of terminating employees with grace and dignity is a nuanced skill that many leaders struggle to master. My journey, encapsulated in this book, is rooted in over two decades of diverse experiences across various industries and roles. From spearheading HR initiatives at The Home Depot to driving strategic growth and culture development at Western Window Systems, and leading Sales and Marketing for a large construction company.

My experiences have taught me that terminating an employee, often viewed as a purely administrative or even cold-hearted task, can in fact be handled in a way that preserves the individual's dignity and even provides a foundation for future growth.

I have witnessed firsthand how the mishandling of terminations can not only damage a former employee's morale but also impact team dynamics and the company's reputation. Conversely, I have also experienced the profound impact that a respectful and empathetic approach to termination can have.

Whether it was reducing staff turnover or reorganizing the workforce, the principles of grace and dignity were always at the forefront of my strategies. The value of terminating with grace and dignity cannot be overstated. It not only speaks volumes about a company's culture and values but also about the leader's character.

It is my hope that this book will not only guide you in your professional endeavors but also inspire you to lead with empathy, integrity, and, above all, a deep respect for the dignity of every person you encounter in your role.

- Robert Robichaud, MSHRM, SHRM-CP, PHR

Table Of Contents

Chapter 1 - Understanding the Importance of Firing with Grace and Dignity

The Consequences of Mishandling Employee Terminations

In the realm of business management, there are few tasks more challenging and emotionally charged than terminating an employee. Whether it is due to poor performance, misconduct, or a company-wide downsizing, the act of letting someone go can have far-reaching consequences if mishandled. This subchapter explores the potential repercussions of mishandling employee terminations and emphasizes the importance of approaching this sensitive task with compassion and respect.

Mishandling employee terminations can lead to a toxic work environment. When employees witness a colleague being fired in an unprofessional or disrespectful manner, it erodes trust and causes anxiety among the remaining staff. This can result in decreased productivity, increased turnover, and a general sense of unease within the organization. Furthermore, word travels fast in the professional world, and news of a mishandled termination can damage a company's reputation, making it more difficult to attract and retain top talent.

Secondly, mishandled terminations can have legal ramifications. If an employee feels they have been wrongfully terminated or treated unfairly during the process, they may pursue legal action against the company. This can result in costly lawsuits, damage to the company's finances and reputation, and a drain on valuable time and resources. By ensuring that terminations are handled with compassion and respect, managers and HR professionals can minimize the risk of legal consequences and protect the company's interests.

Furthermore, mishandling employee terminations can have a profound impact on the mental and emotional well-being of both the terminated employee and those involved in the process. Being fired is often a traumatic experience for individuals, and the manner in which it is handled can either exacerbate or alleviate their pain. By approaching terminations with empathy and providing necessary support, managers and HR professionals can help ease the emotional burden on all parties involved.

Mishandling employee terminations can have far-reaching consequences for organizations, employees, and managers alike. It is imperative that managers, business owners, and HR professionals understand the potential negative outcomes of mishandling such delicate situations. By implementing a compassionate and respectful approach to employee terminations, organizations can maintain a positive work environment, mitigate legal risks, and prioritize the well-being of all involved parties. The Graceful Goodbye - Firing with Compassion and Respect serves as a valuable resource for individuals seeking guidance on how to navigate this challenging aspect of management with grace and professionalism.

The Benefits of Firing with Compassion and Respect

In today's corporate world, the task of firing an employee is often dreaded by managers and business owners alike. It is a difficult and uncomfortable responsibility that can leave a lasting impact on both the terminated employee and the individuals involved in the process. However, there is a better way to handle this delicate situation – firing with compassion and respect. This subchapter explores the numerous benefits of adopting this approach when it comes to employee terminations.

Firing with compassion and respect is not only beneficial for the departing employee but also for the remaining team members. When an employee is let go with dignity, it sends a message to the entire workforce that their contributions are valued and respected. This can boost morale, foster a positive work environment, and increase employee loyalty. By demonstrating compassion and respect during the termination process, managers and business owners show their commitment to treating employees fairly and ethically.

Firing with compassion and respect can also enhance the employer's reputation both internally and externally. Word travels fast, and how an organization handles employee terminations can significantly impact its image. By prioritizing compassion and respect, businesses can establish themselves as employers of choice, attracting top talent and cultivating a positive brand perception. This can lead to improved recruitment efforts and ultimately, better business performance.

Additionally, firing with compassion and respect can minimize legal risks for organizations. When an employee feels they have been treated unfairly or disrespectfully during the termination process, they may be more inclined to take legal action. By ensuring that terminations are conducted in a compassionate and respectful manner, employers can mitigate the chances of facing costly lawsuits and damage to their reputation.

Lastly, firing with compassion and respect allows for a smoother transition for both the departing employee and the organization. By providing support, guidance, and assistance during the termination process, managers and human resource professionals can help the employee navigate their next steps more effectively. This can include providing references, offering career guidance, or connecting them with potential job opportunities. Such assistance not only benefits the departing employee but also ensures a positive experience for the employer and the remaining workforce.

Firing with compassion and respect yields numerous benefits for managers, business owners, and human resource professionals. By adopting this approach, organizations can foster a positive work environment, enhance their reputation, minimize legal risks, and facilitate a smoother transition for all parties involved. In "The Graceful Goodbye - Firing with Compassion and Respect," readers will gain valuable insights and practical strategies to incorporate this approach into their organizations, making employee terminations a more compassionate and respectful process.

The Legal Responsibilities For USA Based Employer's, WARN Act, Unemployment, Notification Periods

The Legal Responsibilities for USA Based Employers - WARN Act, Unemployment, Notification Periods

As a manager, business owner, or human resource professional, it is crucial to understand the legal responsibilities associated with terminating an employee in the United States. Firing an employee is never an easy task, but it is possible to handle the situation with compassion and respect while adhering to the legal framework. In this subchapter, we will explore the key legal aspects that employers must consider when terminating an employee - the WARN Act, unemployment benefits, and notification periods.

The first important law to be aware of is the Worker Adjustment and Retraining Notification (WARN) Act. This federal law requires employers with 100 or more employees to provide at least 60 days' notice in advance of a plant closing or mass layoff. Failure to comply with the WARN Act can result in severe penalties and legal consequences. Understanding the specific requirements of the WARN Act is crucial to ensure compliance and avoid potential legal issues.

Another crucial consideration is the impact of termination on an employee's eligibility for unemployment benefits. Each state has its own regulations regarding unemployment compensation, but in general, employees who are terminated without fault may be eligible to receive unemployment benefits. It is important to provide accurate and timely information to employees about their eligibility and assist them in navigating the unemployment claims process.

Additionally, employers must be aware of the notification periods required by law before terminating an employee. While the specific requirements may vary, providing advance notice to employees helps them plan and adjust to the impending job loss. This demonstrates compassion and respect for employees during an already challenging time.

In summary, understanding the legal responsibilities associated with employee termination is crucial for managers, business owners, and human resource professionals. The WARN Act, unemployment benefits, and notification periods are key factors to consider when navigating the process of firing an employee. By being knowledgeable about these legal aspects, employers can ensure compliance, maintain respectful relationships with employees, and minimize potential legal risks. The Graceful Goodbye - Firing with Compassion and Respect aims to provide guidance and insights on how to handle employee termination in a compassionate and legally compliant manner, ultimately benefiting both the employer and the employee.

Chapter 2 - Preparing for a Graceful Goodbye

Assessing the Need for Termination

The decision to terminate an employee is never an easy one. It is often associated with negative emotions and can have a significant impact on both the individual being let go and the overall dynamics of the workplace. However, there are times when it becomes necessary to part ways with an employee, and it is essential to approach this process with compassion and respect. In this subchapter, we will explore the importance of assessing the need for termination and provide guidance to managers, business owners, and human resource professionals on how to fire an employee with compassion and respect.

Before initiating the termination process, it is crucial to thoroughly evaluate the reasons behind this decision. Assessing the need for termination involves examining various factors, such as performance issues, behavioral problems, and the impact on the team and the organization. It is essential to determine whether the employee's challenges can be resolved through coaching, training, or other interventions. By conducting a comprehensive assessment, you can ensure that termination is truly the best course of action and that all other options have been explored.

One key aspect of assessing the need for termination is evaluating the employee's performance. Are they consistently failing to meet expectations or unable to perform their job duties effectively? Are their actions causing significant harm to the team or the company's reputation? If these issues persist despite efforts to address them, termination may be necessary to maintain the productivity and morale of the workforce.

Another crucial factor to consider is the employee's behavior. If their conduct is disruptive, disrespectful, or in violation of company policies, it can create a toxic work environment. In such cases, termination may be required to protect the well-being and safety of other employees.

It is important to assess the impact of an employee's performance or behavior on the overall team and organization. If their actions are negatively affecting the team's dynamics, productivity, or customer satisfaction, it may be necessary to terminate their employment to maintain a healthy working environment.

However, assessing the need for termination should not be a hasty decision. It is essential to gather all relevant information, document performance or behavioral issues, and seek input from relevant stakeholders. By taking a thoughtful and thorough approach, you can ensure that your decision is fair, objective, and well-justified.

Assessing the need for termination is a critical step in the process of firing an employee with compassion and respect. By evaluating performance, behavior, and the impact on the team and organization, you can make an informed decision that aligns with the best interests of all parties involved. It is essential to approach this process with empathy and transparency, providing support and resources to the employee throughout the termination process. By doing so, you can uphold the values of compassion and respect while also safeguarding the success and well-being of your team and organization.

Progressive Discipline Model

The Progressive Discipline Model is a crucial approach for managers, business owners, and human resource professionals to effectively handle employee termination with compassion and respect. It provides a structured framework that empowers employers to address performance or behavioral issues while giving employees opportunities to improve and rectify their shortcomings.

The cornerstone of the Progressive Discipline Model is fairness and objectivity. It enables employers to handle disciplinary actions in a consistent manner, ensuring that all employees are treated equally and that no bias or favoritism exists within the organization. By following this model, managers and HR professionals can maintain transparency throughout the disciplinary process, which facilitates trust and allows employees to understand the reasoning behind the decisions made.

The model operates through a series of escalating steps, commencing with verbal warnings and progressing to written reprimands, suspension, and ultimately, termination. Each step involves clear communication with the employee, outlining the specific concerns, expectations, and consequences of their actions. This open dialogue encourages employees to take responsibility for their behavior and actively participate in their own professional development.

The Progressive Discipline Model recognizes that termination should be the last resort. It emphasizes the importance of offering employees opportunities for improvement and growth, enabling them to rectify their mistakes and reach their full potential. Through coaching, training, and mentorship programs, employers can provide the necessary support for employees to overcome their deficiencies and succeed in their roles.

Adhering to the Progressive Discipline Model not only benefits the employee in question but also the entire organization. By giving individuals the chance to improve, businesses can minimize turnover and retain valuable talent. Additionally, it fosters a positive and inclusive work culture, where employees feel supported and encouraged to reach their highest potential.

The Progressive Discipline Model is an essential tool for managers, business owners, and human resource professionals when navigating the challenging task of terminating an employee. By implementing this model, employers can address performance or behavioral issues with compassion and respect, while maintaining fairness and transparency. Ultimately, it paves the way for a graceful and dignified exit for the employee, while ensuring the continued success and growth of the organization.

Identifying Alternatives to Firing

In the realm of management, there may come a time when the difficult decision of terminating an employee must be made. However, before resorting to firing as the only solution, it is essential for managers, business owners, and human resource professionals to explore alternative options. This subchapter aims to shed light on various alternatives to firing, enabling a graceful goodbye that prioritizes compassion and respect.

One alternative to firing is providing additional training and support to struggling employees. Often, poor performance can be attributed to a lack of proper skills, knowledge, or resources. By investing in training programs, mentoring, or coaching, managers can empower employees to improve their performance and grow within their roles. This approach not only benefits the individual employee but also contributes to the overall success of the organization.

Another alternative is job restructuring or reassignment. Sometimes, an employee may be struggling in their current position due to a poor fit between their skills and the demands of the role. In such cases, managers can consider reassigning the employee to a different department or project that aligns better with their strengths and interests. By leveraging their existing talents, employees can excel in new roles and contribute significantly to the organization's goals.

Implementing a performance improvement plan (PIP) is yet another alternative to firing. A PIP sets clear expectations and goals for the employee, outlining areas for improvement and providing a timeline for achieving these objectives. This structured approach allows managers to monitor progress and provide necessary support along the way. In many cases, employees respond positively to this opportunity for growth and succeed in meeting the established expectations.

Fostering open communication is crucial when identifying alternatives to firing. Managers should create a safe space for employees to express their concerns, challenges, and potential solutions. Through dialogue, managers may discover underlying issues that can be resolved through mediation, conflict resolution, or implementing changes to work conditions. This proactive approach can salvage relationships and prevent the need for termination.

Ultimately, identifying alternatives to firing requires creativity, empathy, and a commitment to the growth and well-being of both the employee and the organization. By exploring these alternatives, managers, business owners, and human resource professionals can navigate the delicate process of firing with compassion and respect, ensuring a graceful goodbye for all parties involved.

Understanding Legal and Ethical Considerations

In the modern workplace, the process of terminating an employee is fraught with legal and ethical considerations. As managers, business owners, and human resource professionals, it is essential to approach the task of firing an employee with compassion and respect. This subchapter aims to provide a comprehensive understanding of the legal and ethical aspects involved in the termination process.

From a legal perspective, it is crucial to be well-versed in the employment laws and regulations that govern the termination process. This includes understanding the legal requirements for terminating an employee, such as providing proper notice or severance pay where applicable. Additionally, knowledge of anti-discrimination laws is vital to ensure that the termination is not based on any protected characteristics, such as race, gender, religion, or disability. Familiarity with privacy laws and confidentiality obligations is also essential to safeguard the employee's personal information during and after the termination process.

Ethical considerations are equally important when terminating an employee. Firing someone is a significant life event that can have a profound impact on the individual's self-esteem, financial stability, and overall well-being. Therefore, it is essential to approach the process with empathy, sensitivity, and respect. Communicating openly and honestly with the employee, providing clear reasons for the termination, and offering support in transitioning to new employment or outplacement services are ethical practices that can minimize the negative impact of the termination.

Moreover, it is crucial to consider the implications of the termination on the remaining employees and the workplace culture. Terminating an employee should be seen as a last resort, after all other alternatives, such as performance improvement plans or reassignment, have been exhausted. This ensures that the decision to fire is fair and reasonable, avoiding potential resentment or distrust from the remaining employees.

To navigate the legal and ethical considerations successfully, it is advisable to consult with legal professionals or HR experts who specialize in employment law. They can provide guidance on legal compliance, offer insights into best practices, and help develop termination policies that align with the organization's values and goals.

Understanding the legal and ethical considerations involved in firing an employee is essential for managers, business owners, and HR professionals. By adhering to legal requirements, treating employees with compassion and respect, and considering the impact on the workplace, organizations can conduct terminations in a manner that preserves dignity and upholds ethical standards.

Case Study 1 - The Right Way and The Wrong Way to Terminate

In the world of business, terminating an employee is a difficult and often uncomfortable task. It is a situation that managers, business owners, and human resource professionals encounter at some point in their careers. However, it is crucial to approach this process with compassion and respect, as it can have a significant impact on both the individual being let go and the overall company culture.

This case study explores two contrasting scenarios - the right way and the wrong way to terminate an employee. By examining these examples, managers, business owners, and human resource professionals can gain valuable insights into how to handle such situations with grace and empathy.

The Wrong Way -
In this particular case, the employee was called into a meeting with the manager, without any prior notice or indication that termination was on the table. The manager was cold and distant, failing to provide any feedback or explanation for the decision. The employee was left feeling confused, humiliated, and unsupported. The lack of compassion and respect in this approach not only damaged the individual's self-esteem but also harmed the company's reputation and employee morale.

The Right Way -
Contrastingly, in this scenario, the manager scheduled a private meeting with the employee, allowing time for both parties to prepare. During the meeting, the manager expressed appreciation for the employee's contributions and acknowledged the difficulty of the situation. The reasons for the termination were clearly communicated, and the manager offered support, such as career counseling or recommendations for other job opportunities. The employee was treated with empathy, dignity, and respect, which helped to soften the blow and maintain a positive relationship.

This case study highlights the importance of adopting a compassionate and respectful approach when terminating an employee. By following the right way, managers, business owners, and human resource professionals can minimize the negative impact on both the individual and the organization. Firing an employee is never an easy task, but when handled with grace, it can be an opportunity for growth and development for all parties involved.

In conclusion, "The Graceful Goodbye - Firing with Compassion and Respect" emphasizes the significance of treating employees with empathy, even in challenging situations. This subchapter provides valuable insights into the right way and the wrong way to terminate an employee, equipping managers, business owners, and human resource professionals with the necessary tools to approach these situations with compassion and respect. By fostering a culture of empathy and understanding, organizations can build stronger relationships with their employees and maintain a positive reputation in the industry.

Chapter 3 - Creating a Supportive Environment

Cultivating a Positive Company Culture

Creating and maintaining a positive company culture is crucial for the success and growth of any organization. It not only boosts employee morale and productivity but also attracts and retains top talent.

In this subchapter, we will explore effective strategies for cultivating a positive company culture, which will ultimately contribute to a compassionate and respectful approach when it comes to firing employees.

First and foremost, fostering open communication is paramount. Encourage a culture where employees feel comfortable expressing their thoughts, concerns, and ideas. Implement regular feedback sessions and maintain an open-door policy, ensuring that everyone's voice is heard. This promotes transparency, trust, and collaboration, which are essential elements of a positive company culture.

Next, emphasize the importance of work-life balance. Encourage employees to maintain a healthy equilibrium between their personal and professional lives. Provide flexible work arrangements, promote wellness programs, and organize team-building activities to foster a sense of community and support among the workforce. When employees feel valued and supported, they are more likely to contribute positively to the company's overall culture.

Furthermore, recognize and reward outstanding performance. Implement a comprehensive employee recognition program that acknowledges and appreciates individuals who go above and beyond in their roles. Celebrate achievements, both big and small, and publicly recognize employees for their hard work and dedication. This not only boosts morale but also motivates others to strive for excellence.

Another crucial aspect of cultivating a positive company culture is promoting diversity and inclusion. Embrace and celebrate differences among employees, fostering an environment where everyone feels included and valued. Implement diversity training programs, establish diversity and inclusion committees, and create opportunities for employees to learn from one another. Embracing diversity not only enhances creativity and problem-solving but also contributes to a more compassionate and respectful workplace.

Managers and business owners must embody the principles they wish to see in their employees. Demonstrate compassion, respect, and fairness in all interactions. Be approachable, listen attentively, and provide constructive feedback. Your behavior and attitude will set the tone for the entire organization.

By cultivating a positive company culture, you lay the groundwork for firing employees with compassion and respect. When such unfortunate circumstances arise, employees will already be aware of the organization's values and understand that difficult decisions are made with careful consideration. This approach allows for smoother transitions, maintains professionalism, and preserves the dignity of all parties involved.

Communicating Expectations and Performance Standards

In the realm of managing employees, it is crucial to establish clear expectations and performance standards. This subchapter of "The Graceful Goodbye - Firing with Compassion and Respect" delves into the significance of effective communication in this regard. Aimed at managers, business owners, and human resource professionals, this section offers valuable insights on how to fire an employee with compassion and respect by focusing on establishing and communicating expectations and performance standards.

Setting clear expectations is the foundation of any successful working relationship. When employees know exactly what is expected of them, they are more likely to perform at their best. Managers play a pivotal role in clearly articulating these expectations from the onset. By providing a detailed job description, defining key performance indicators, and outlining specific goals and targets, managers can ensure that employees understand what is required of them.

However, communication is a two-way street. It is equally important for managers to listen to their employees' perspectives and concerns. Regular feedback sessions, performance evaluations, and open-door policies can facilitate effective communication channels between managers and employees. By actively engaging in dialogue, managers can gain valuable insights into their employees' challenges, aspirations, and potential areas for growth.

Performance standards should also be communicated transparently. Employees need to understand the metrics by which their performance will be evaluated. This ensures fairness and consistency in the assessment process. Additionally, managers should provide regular updates on performance, highlighting areas of improvement and acknowledging outstanding achievements. Constructive criticism and guidance should be given promptly, allowing employees to adjust their actions and behaviors accordingly.

In this subchapter, "The Graceful Goodbye - Firing with Compassion and Respect" emphasizes the importance of communicating expectations and performance standards throughout the employee's tenure. By doing so, managers can reduce the likelihood of surprises or misunderstandings that may lead to the need for termination. Furthermore, effective communication fosters an environment of trust, where employees feel supported and valued, even during challenging times.

This subchapter serves as a comprehensive guide for managers, business owners, and human resource professionals on how to fire an employee with compassion and respect. By prioritizing clear communication of expectations and performance standards, managers can create a positive and productive workplace culture, while minimizing the need for termination.

Providing Ongoing Feedback and Coaching

In the journey of managing employees, providing ongoing feedback and coaching is an essential aspect that ensures growth and development within the organization. This subchapter delves into the significance of regularly communicating with employees, offering constructive feedback, and providing coaching to help them improve their performance. By implementing these strategies, managers, business owners, and human resource professionals can create a more compassionate and respectful environment, even in the challenging task of firing an employee.

Regular communication and feedback serve as the backbone of a productive work environment. It is crucial for managers to provide clear expectations to employees and establish open lines of communication. By regularly checking in with employees, managers can identify any issues or concerns early on, preventing them from escalating into major problems. Moreover, consistent feedback allows employees to understand their strengths and areas for improvement, fostering continuous growth.

Constructive feedback plays a vital role in shaping employee performance. Managers should approach feedback as an opportunity to guide employees, rather than criticizing or demoralizing them. By focusing on specific behaviors or actions, managers can provide actionable recommendations for improvement. It is essential to express feedback in a compassionate and respectful manner, emphasizing the employee's potential and highlighting areas where they can excel. This approach helps employees view feedback as a means to enhance their skills and contribute more effectively to the organization.

Coaching is another powerful tool for employee development. Managers should invest time and effort in understanding each employee's unique strengths and weaknesses. By tailoring coaching sessions to individual needs, managers can effectively guide employees towards achieving their goals. This personalized approach demonstrates a commitment to employee growth and fosters a sense of trust between the manager and employee.

By incorporating ongoing feedback and coaching into their management style, managers, business owners, and human resource professionals can navigate the challenging task of firing an employee with compassion and respect. When an employee's performance consistently falls below expectations despite efforts to support their growth, termination may become necessary. However, by providing ongoing feedback and coaching, managers can ensure that the employee understands the reasons for termination and provide them with resources or recommendations for their future career.

Providing ongoing feedback and coaching is a crucial aspect of effective management. By implementing these strategies, managers can create a compassionate and respectful work environment that fosters growth and development. Even in the difficult task of terminating an employee, ongoing feedback and coaching ensure that the process is conducted with compassion and respect.

Chapter 4 - Planning and Conducting a Compassionate Termination Meeting

Developing an Effective Termination Plan

In the world of business, sometimes tough decisions have to be made. One of the most challenging tasks for managers, business owners, and human resource professionals is terminating an employee. However, it is crucial to handle such situations with compassion and respect. This subchapter aims to guide managers through the process of creating an effective termination plan, ensuring that the process is conducted in a graceful and respectful manner.

1. Assess the Situation - Before initiating the termination process, it is essential to evaluate the circumstances surrounding the employee's performance or behavior. Clearly outline the reasons for termination and gather all the necessary documentation to support your decision. This step will help ensure that the termination is fair and justified.

2. Plan the Conversation - When delivering the news to the employee, it is crucial to plan the conversation carefully. Choose an appropriate time and location for the meeting, ensuring privacy and minimal distractions. Prepare a script or outline to guide the conversation, focusing on the facts and avoiding personal attacks. This will help maintain a respectful and professional atmosphere.

3. Communicate Clearly and Compassionately - During the termination meeting, it is vital to communicate the decision clearly and compassionately. Start the conversation by expressing appreciation for the employee's contributions, emphasizing that the termination is based on specific performance or behavior issues. Provide honest feedback and offer suggestions for improvement, if applicable. Allow the employee to express their thoughts and feelings, but remain firm in the decision.

4. Provide Support - Even though termination can be difficult for both parties involved, it is essential to offer support to the employee during this transition. Provide information about severance packages, outplacement services, or any other resources that can assist them in finding new employment. Ensure that all necessary paperwork, such as termination letters and final paychecks, are prepared and provided promptly.

5. Maintain Confidentiality and Minimize Disruption - After the termination, it is crucial to maintain confidentiality to protect both the employee's privacy and the reputation of the organization. Communicate the news to the remaining team members in a professional and sensitive manner, without disclosing unnecessary details. Ensure that the employee's departure does not cause any unnecessary disruption to the overall workflow.

By following these steps and developing an effective termination plan, managers, business owners, and human resource professionals can navigate the challenging process of firing an employee with compassion and respect. Remember, treating employees with dignity even during difficult times reflects positively on the organization's culture and reputation, fostering an environment of trust and fairness.

Who Should do The Termination and Who Should be Present During

In the delicate process of terminating an employee, it is essential to approach the situation with compassion and respect. As managers, business owners, and human resource professionals, it is our responsibility to handle these situations with utmost care, ensuring that the employee's dignity is preserved while protecting the interests of the organization.

In this subchapter, we will discuss the crucial factors to consider when determining who should carry out the termination and who should be present during the process.

Firstly, the person responsible for conducting the termination should ideally be the employee's immediate supervisor or manager. This individual is likely to have the most direct knowledge of the employee's performance and conduct, making them best equipped to communicate the reasons for the termination in a clear and concise manner. Additionally, having a familiar face deliver the news can help ease the employee's potential emotional distress, as they may feel more comfortable discussing their concerns or asking questions.

However, it is important to note that not all managers or supervisors possess the necessary skills or temperament to handle termination conversations effectively. In such cases, it may be wise to involve a human resource professional who has experience in managing these difficult conversations. HR professionals can provide guidance and support to both the manager delivering the news and the employee receiving it, ensuring that the process is handled compassionately and respectfully.

Furthermore, during the termination process, it is crucial to determine who should be present in the room. While it may be tempting to have multiple individuals present as witnesses or for support, it is generally advised to keep the meeting as private and confidential as possible.

Having too many people in the room can overwhelm the employee, making it more challenging for them to process the information and respond appropriately. However, it is essential to have at least one additional person present to serve as a witness and provide support to the employee during this difficult time. This person can also assist in taking notes and documenting the conversation, ensuring that all details are accurately recorded.

Terminating an employee with compassion and respect requires careful consideration of who should conduct the termination and who should be present during the process.

The immediate supervisor or manager is often the best choice for delivering the news, but involving a human resource professional may be necessary in some cases. Keeping the meeting as private as possible is advised, with one additional person present to serve as support and witness. By approaching terminations with empathy and sensitivity, we can ensure that even in challenging circumstances, the graceful goodbye is achieved.

Choosing the Right Location and Timing

In the delicate process of terminating an employee, there are numerous factors to consider to ensure a graceful goodbye. One crucial aspect that often gets overlooked is choosing the right location and timing for the termination meeting. The location and timing can greatly impact the employee's experience and ultimately influence the level of compassion and respect shown during this difficult time.

When selecting a location for the termination meeting, it is essential to prioritize privacy and discretion. Find a space where the conversation can remain confidential and uninterrupted. This could be a private office, a meeting room, or any other secluded area within the workplace. By providing a confidential setting, you create a safe space for the employee to express their emotions and process the news without the fear of public humiliation.

Timing is equally significant when it comes to delivering the news compassionately. Avoid terminating an employee on a Friday or just before a holiday, as this may intensify the emotional impact and leave the individual feeling isolated during a time when social support may be limited. Instead, choose a day early in the week when the employee can explore their options promptly and begin their job search with the support of employment agencies and resources.

Additionally, consider the employee's personal circumstances when deciding on the timing. While there may never be an ideal time to terminate someone, try to be mindful of any significant life events they may be experiencing, such as a death in the family or personal illness. Showing empathy by acknowledging these circumstances and providing appropriate support can go a long way in demonstrating compassion during this challenging time.

By carefully selecting the location and timing for the termination meeting, you create an environment that is conducive to compassion and respect. This approach allows the employee to maintain their dignity and minimizes the potential for humiliation or distress. Remember that while the decision to terminate an employee may be necessary for the organization's needs, the process can still be conducted with empathy and understanding.

As managers, business owners, and human resource professionals, it is our responsibility to uphold the values of compassion and respect throughout the termination process. By considering the location and timing of the termination meeting, we can ensure a graceful goodbye that supports the employee's transition and helps them move forward with dignity.

Crafting a Compassionate Termination Script

When it comes to the delicate task of terminating an employee, it is essential to handle the conversation with compassion and respect. The way you communicate this news can have a profound impact on the individual's well-being and the overall morale of your team. In this subchapter, we will discuss the art of crafting a compassionate termination script that ensures a graceful goodbye while maintaining professionalism.

The first step in crafting a compassionate termination script is to approach the conversation with empathy. Put yourself in the employee's shoes and consider the impact this news will have on their life. Begin the conversation by expressing appreciation for their contributions and acknowledging their efforts. This will help set a positive tone and show that you value their work.

Next, provide clear and honest feedback about the reasons behind the termination. Be specific, but avoid personal attacks or harsh language. Focus on the performance or behavioral issues that led to this decision, and offer examples to support your points. Remember to deliver this feedback in a constructive manner, providing suggestions for improvement or resources that may be available to help them in their next steps.

It is crucial to allow the employee to share their thoughts and feelings during this difficult conversation. Actively listen to their responses, and validate their emotions without becoming defensive. This will help them feel heard and respected, even in this challenging situation. Additionally, be prepared to answer any questions they may have, providing honest and transparent responses.

To ensure a compassionate departure, offer resources and support to help the employee transition smoothly. This may include providing information on career counseling services, outplacement assistance, or unemployment benefits. Demonstrating that you genuinely care about their future can make a significant difference in their perception of the termination.

Lastly, end the conversation on a positive note. Express your sincere wishes for their future success and emphasize that this decision is not a reflection of their worth as an individual. Offer to provide a reference or assist them in their job search if appropriate. A compassionate termination script should leave the employee feeling respected, supported, and empowered to move forward.

Crafting a compassionate termination script is crucial for managers, business owners, and human resource professionals. By approaching the conversation with empathy, providing honest feedback, offering resources, and ending on a positive note, you can ensure a graceful goodbye while maintaining professionalism. Remember, firing an employee with compassion and respect is not only ethical but also essential for the well-being of your team and the overall success of your organization.

Chapter 5 - Delivering the Message with Empathy and Respect

Active Listening and Empathetic Communication

In the realm of managing employees, there inevitably comes a time when difficult decisions need to be made. One of the most challenging aspects of being a manager, business owner, or human resource professional is having to fire an employee. However, it is possible to approach this difficult task with compassion and respect. This subchapter aims to provide valuable insights on active listening and empathetic communication, helping managers navigate the process of letting an employee go while preserving their dignity.

Active listening is an essential skill that allows for effective communication and understanding. When engaged in the process of firing an employee, it is crucial to listen attentively, without interruption or judgment. By actively listening, managers can gain valuable insights into the employee's perspective, emotions, and concerns. This not only helps in understanding the situation better but also establishes a foundation for empathetic communication.

Empathetic communication is the ability to convey understanding, compassion, and respect. When firing an employee, it is vital to approach the conversation with empathy, acknowledging the impact it may have on their life. By expressing empathy, managers demonstrate that they genuinely care about the employee's well-being and are committed to treating them with dignity. This can greatly alleviate the stress and anxiety often associated with termination.

To effectively communicate empathetically, it is essential to choose words and tone carefully. Managers should focus on using language that is respectful, clear, and compassionate. Providing honest feedback while expressing gratitude for the employee's contributions can help soften the blow and maintain a positive relationship, even during a difficult time.

Furthermore, non-verbal cues play a significant role in empathetic communication. Maintaining eye contact, using open body language, and displaying genuine concern through facial expressions can enhance the message of empathy and understanding. These non-verbal cues reassure the employee that they are being heard and valued throughout the process.

Active listening and empathetic communication are indispensable tools when it comes to firing an employee with compassion and respect. By actively listening, managers gain valuable insights into the employee's perspective, facilitating empathetic communication. Through empathetic communication, managers can convey understanding, compassion, and respect, ensuring that the employee's dignity is preserved throughout the termination process. Developing and honing these skills will allow managers, business owners, and human resource professionals to navigate the difficult task of firing an employee gracefully and with utmost compassion.

Acknowledging Employee Contributions and Efforts

In the realm of business management, acknowledging the contributions and efforts of employees is an essential aspect of fostering a positive and productive work environment.

It not only boosts employee morale and motivation but also cultivates a sense of loyalty and commitment towards the organization. In this subchapter, we will explore the significance of acknowledging employee contributions and efforts, and provide practical strategies for doing so with compassion and respect.

Recognizing the efforts and achievements of employees is crucial in building a culture of appreciation within the workplace. When employees feel valued and appreciated, they are more likely to engage in their work, exhibit higher levels of job satisfaction, and go the extra mile to achieve organizational goals. Managers, business owners, and human resource professionals must understand the power of acknowledging employee contributions as a means of creating a supportive and inclusive atmosphere.

One effective way to acknowledge employee contributions is through regular and meaningful feedback. Providing constructive feedback that highlights individuals' strengths and areas for improvement not only helps them grow professionally but also shows that their efforts are recognized and valued. Moreover, recognizing and celebrating milestones, achievements, and exceptional performances publicly can amplify the impact of acknowledgment, fostering a sense of pride and accomplishment among employees.

Another approach to acknowledging employee contributions is through rewards and recognition programs. These can range from simple gestures such as verbal praise and thank-you notes to more formal recognition programs, such as Employee of the Month awards or performance-based bonuses. By implementing such programs, managers and HR professionals can ensure that outstanding contributions do not go unnoticed and are duly rewarded, motivating employees to continue excelling in their roles.

Furthermore, it is essential to create an open and transparent communication channel where employees feel comfortable sharing their thoughts and ideas.

Actively listening to their perspectives, seeking their input, and involving them in decision-making processes not only acknowledges their contributions but also empowers them to take ownership of their work and contribute to the organization's success.

Acknowledging employee contributions and efforts is vital for creating a compassionate and respectful work environment. By implementing strategies such as providing regular feedback, recognizing achievements, and fostering open communication, managers, business owners, and HR professionals can ensure that employees feel valued and appreciated. By doing so, they not only contribute to the well-being and satisfaction of employees but also enhance the overall productivity and success of the organization.

Handling Emotional Reactions and Offering Support

When it comes to the delicate task of terminating an employee, it is crucial for managers, business owners, and human resource professionals to approach the situation with compassion and respect. This subchapter aims to provide valuable insights and strategies on how to handle emotional reactions during the termination process while offering essential support to the employee being let go.

Emotions can run high during a termination, causing stress and anxiety for both parties involved. As a manager, it is essential to approach the situation with empathy and understanding. Begin by creating a supportive environment where the employee feels comfortable expressing their emotions. Assure them that their feelings are valid and encourage open communication throughout the process.

It is important to remember that termination affects not only the employee but also their colleagues. Addressing the emotional impact on the team is equally crucial. Acknowledge the emotions that may arise in the workplace and provide guidance to other employees on how to cope with the changes. This will help maintain a positive work environment and prevent any unnecessary disruptions.

Offering support to the employee being terminated is pivotal in facilitating a graceful goodbye. Provide them with resources and information about outplacement services, career counseling, or job placement agencies. These resources can assist them in finding new employment opportunities, boosting their confidence during this challenging period.

Consider providing a severance package or other financial assistance to ease their transition. This gesture demonstrates your commitment to their well-being and can help alleviate some of the financial burdens they may face.

Throughout the termination process, it is crucial to remain sensitive to the employee's emotions and maintain open lines of communication. Regular check-ins after the termination can provide an opportunity for them to express any concerns or questions they may have. This ongoing support will help them navigate this difficult period and can contribute to a smoother transition.

Handling emotional reactions and offering support during the termination process is essential for managers, business owners, and human resource professionals. By approaching the situation with compassion and respect, providing resources, and maintaining open communication, you can ensure a graceful goodbye that upholds the dignity of the employee being terminated. Remember, treating employees with empathy and support is not only the right thing to do but also contributes to a positive company culture and reputation.

Chapter 6 - Assisting Employees in Transition

Offering Career Counseling and Job Search Support

In any organization, the decision to let go of an employee can be a challenging and emotionally charged experience. However, it is essential to handle such situations with compassion and respect, ensuring that the employee's dignity and well-being are prioritized.

As managers, business owners, and human resource professionals, it is our responsibility to provide support during this difficult transition. This subchapter aims to guide you on how to offer career counseling and job search support to those who have been let go.

Career counseling plays a vital role in helping employees navigate their professional journey and find new employment opportunities. By offering career counseling services, you demonstrate your commitment to your employees' growth and development beyond their tenure with your organization. This support can include helping them identify their skills, strengths, and interests, exploring alternative career paths, and creating a personalized action plan for their job search.

One effective way to provide career counseling is by partnering with external career coaches or counselors. These professionals bring expertise and objectivity to the process, ensuring that employees receive the guidance they need. Consider establishing relationships with reputable career counseling firms or individuals who can provide one-on-one coaching sessions or group workshops. By offering these resources, you equip your former employees with the tools they need to navigate the job market successfully.

Additionally, job search support is a crucial component of the transition process. Help your former employees in their job search by providing them with resources such as resume writing assistance, interview preparation workshops, and networking opportunities. Encourage them to utilize online job boards, professional networking platforms, and industry-specific websites to explore potential job openings. By equipping them with these tools, you empower them to take charge of their career transition.

Remember, offering career counseling and job search support does not stop at merely providing resources. It requires ongoing communication and follow-up. Regularly check in with your former employees to offer guidance, answer questions, and provide emotional support during what can be a challenging time. This ongoing support demonstrates your commitment to their well-being and helps maintain a positive relationship even after their departure from your organization.

By offering career counseling and job search support, you embody the values of compassion and respect throughout the employee termination process. Your commitment to their professional growth and well-being will not only benefit them but also enhance your reputation as an employer who values their employees' long-term success.

Providing Resources for Financial Assistance

One of the most challenging aspects of terminating an employee is the potential impact it may have on their financial stability. As managers, business owners, and human resource professionals, it is our responsibility to approach this difficult situation with compassion and respect. In this subchapter, we will explore the various resources available to assist employees during their transition period, ensuring they receive the support they need.

1. Severance Packages - Consider offering a severance package as a gesture of goodwill and financial assistance. Tailor the package based on the employee's length of service, position, and other relevant factors. Providing a financial cushion can help alleviate some of the immediate financial stress they may face.

2. Unemployment Benefits - Educate employees about the process of applying for unemployment benefits. Provide them with the necessary information and contacts to ensure a smooth transition into this government assistance program. This resource can provide temporary financial relief while they search for new employment.

3. Outplacement Services - Engage the services of an outplacement agency to support the terminated employee in finding new job opportunities. These agencies offer career counseling, resume writing assistance, interview coaching, and job search resources. By providing access to such services, you are demonstrating your commitment to their future success.

4. Financial Planning and Counseling - Offer access to financial planning and counseling services to help employees manage their finances during the transition period. These professionals can provide guidance on budgeting, debt management, and future financial planning, ensuring the employee feels supported beyond the termination process.

5. Employee Assistance Programs (EAPs) - Highlight the availability of EAPs to employees, emphasizing that these programs can provide confidential counseling and support. EAPs often offer financial planning advice, mental health resources, and guidance for managing stress during challenging times.

6. Networking Opportunities - Encourage terminated employees to network and connect with industry professionals who might have job leads or valuable advice. Facilitate introductions, provide access to online networking platforms, or host networking events to foster connections that can help them land their next position.

By providing these resources for financial assistance, you are not only showing compassion and respect but also investing in the long-term well-being of your employees. Remember, the way you handle terminations can impact your company's reputation and employer brand. By demonstrating your commitment to supporting employees during their transition, you foster a culture of empathy and compassion that will be recognized and appreciated by both current and future employees.

Connecting Employees with Outplacement Services

One of the most crucial aspects of firing an employee with compassion and respect is ensuring that they are provided with the necessary support to transition into their next career opportunity. Outplacement services play a pivotal role in this process, offering guidance and resources to help employees navigate the job market effectively. By connecting employees with outplacement services, managers, business owners, and human resource professionals can demonstrate their commitment to the well-being of their employees even in difficult times.

Outplacement services provide a range of essential tools and support to employees who have been let go. These services typically include resume writing assistance, interview coaching, job search strategies, and access to networking opportunities. By partnering with reputable outplacement providers, employers can offer their employees a comprehensive suite of services tailored to their individual needs, ensuring a smoother transition and an increased chance of finding new employment.

When connecting employees with outplacement services, it is important to approach the process with empathy and sensitivity. Communicate the decision to terminate the employee's employment with compassion, emphasizing that the company understands the impact this will have on their life and career. Offer reassurance that the organization is committed to supporting them during this challenging time by providing access to outplacement services.

Managers, business owners, and human resource professionals should take the time to explain the benefits of outplacement services to the employee. Highlight how these services can enhance their chances of finding a new job quickly and successfully, and emphasize the value of professional guidance and support during the job search process.

To maximize the effectiveness of outplacement services, it is essential to ensure a seamless transition. Provide employees with detailed information about the outplacement services available to them and how to access them. Consider scheduling a meeting with the outplacement provider to introduce the employee to their designated consultant, fostering a sense of trust and familiarity from the start.

Ultimately, connecting employees with outplacement services is a vital step in the process of firing with compassion and respect. By offering comprehensive support, guidance, and resources to help employees navigate their career transition, managers, business owners, and human resource professionals can demonstrate their commitment to the well-being of their employees, even during challenging times.

Chapter 7 - Maintaining Compassion and Respect After the Termination

Communicating the Departure to the Team

When it comes to letting an employee go, one of the most crucial aspects is effectively communicating the departure to the rest of the team. This subchapter will provide valuable insights and strategies on how managers, business owners, and human resource professionals can handle this challenging task with compassion and respect.

1. Timing is Key -
Timing plays a vital role in communicating the departure to the team. It is essential to inform the team as soon as possible, but also ensure that all necessary details and logistics are in place before the announcement. This helps maintain transparency and avoid any unnecessary rumors or confusion.

2. Plan and Prepare -
Before communicating the departure, it is crucial to plan and prepare your message. Be clear about the reasons for the employee's departure without divulging confidential information. Highlight the employee's contributions and acknowledge their efforts, emphasizing that the decision was not made lightly.

3. Choose the Right Medium -
Selecting the appropriate communication medium is important. While face-to-face meetings are ideal, it may not always be feasible, especially in remote or large organizations. In such cases, consider video conferences or personalized emails to convey the news with a personal touch.

4. Be Honest and Transparent -

Honesty and transparency are key to maintaining trust within the team. Clearly communicate the reasons behind the decision without being overly negative or critical. Provide reassurance that any necessary changes will be handled smoothly and that the team's support is essential during this transition.

5. Address Concerns and Questions -

After delivering the news, be prepared for questions and concerns from the team. Address them honestly and openly, ensuring that all inquiries are handled respectfully. Emphasize the importance of confidentiality and avoid gossip or speculation.

6. Provide Support -

Losing a team member can cause anxiety and uncertainty among the remaining employees. As a manager or HR professional, it is crucial to provide support during this transition. Offer resources, such as counseling or training, to help team members cope with the change and any additional responsibilities.

7. Foster a Positive Environment -

Throughout the transition, emphasize the importance of maintaining a positive and supportive workplace culture. Encourage teamwork, open communication, and provide opportunities for team members to express any concerns or suggestions.

Communicating the departure of an employee to the team requires careful planning, honesty, and compassion. By following these strategies, managers, business owners, and HR professionals can navigate this challenging task while ensuring that the team remains engaged, supported, and motivated during the transition.

Addressing Grief and Emotions in the Workplace

In the fast-paced world of business, it is often easy to overlook the emotional toll that firing an employee can have on both the individual being let go and the remaining members of the team. However, it is crucial for managers, business owners, and human resource professionals to address grief and emotions in the workplace with compassion and respect. By doing so, they can ensure a graceful goodbye and maintain a positive work environment.

Recognizing and acknowledging the emotional impact of termination is the first step in addressing grief in the workplace. Losing a job can be a traumatic experience for anyone, causing feelings of anger, sadness, and even depression. Managers must approach the situation with empathy and understanding, creating a safe space for the employee to express their emotions. This can be achieved through active listening, validating their feelings, and offering support.

Open communication is key when addressing grief and emotions in the workplace. Managers should encourage employees to share their thoughts and concerns, allowing them to process their emotions in a healthy manner. Regular check-ins and one-on-one meetings can provide a platform for individuals to express themselves, ensuring their voices are heard and their needs are addressed.

Providing resources and support is essential in helping employees navigate their emotions during this challenging time. Offering access to counseling services or employee assistance programs can be invaluable for individuals struggling with grief. Additionally, managers can organize workshops or training sessions to educate employees on coping mechanisms and stress management techniques.

Creating a supportive work environment is crucial in addressing grief and emotions. Colleagues should be encouraged to offer support and understanding to their fellow team members who may be going through a difficult time. Promoting a culture of empathy and compassion within the workplace can help ease the emotional burden and foster a sense of unity among employees.

By addressing grief and emotions in the workplace with compassion and respect, managers, business owners, and human resource professionals can ensure a graceful goodbye for employees who are being let go. This not only helps individuals navigate their emotions but also strengthens the overall work environment. By recognizing the emotional impact of termination, fostering open communication, providing resources and support, and creating a supportive work environment, organizations can handle the process of firing an employee with integrity and care.

Supporting the Remaining Team Members

In any organization, when an employee is let go, it can have a ripple effect on the entire team. The remaining team members may experience a range of emotions, from shock and sadness to fear and uncertainty. As a manager, business owner, or human resource professional, it is crucial to provide support and stability to the remaining team members during this challenging time. This subchapter will explore effective strategies for supporting the remaining team members after an employee has been fired, ensuring a graceful goodbye that preserves compassion and respect.

Firstly, open communication is key. Transparency and honesty are essential when addressing the situation with the remaining team members. Organize a team meeting to discuss the departure of the employee, emphasizing that the decision was made after careful consideration and not taken lightly. Provide a clear explanation of the reasons for the termination while maintaining confidentiality and privacy. Address any concerns or questions the team may have, reassuring them of their importance to the organization and their value as individuals.

It is crucial to acknowledge and validate the emotions that the team members may be experiencing. Allow them the space to express their feelings and concerns, and be empathetic towards their reactions. Encourage open dialogue and provide a supportive environment where the team feels comfortable discussing their thoughts and emotions. Offer individual or group counseling sessions if necessary, to ensure that everyone has access to the support they need.

Additionally, it is important to maintain team morale and motivation during this transition. Clearly define the roles and responsibilities of each team member, ensuring that they have a clear understanding of their new expectations. Consider providing additional training or resources to help the team members adapt to any changes resulting from the employee's departure. Recognize and reward their efforts, acknowledging the additional workload they may have taken on. This will not only boost morale but also demonstrate your appreciation for their commitment and dedication.

Lastly, monitor the team dynamics closely. Keep an eye out for any signs of tension or conflict that may arise as a result of the employee's departure. Address any issues promptly, promoting open communication and fostering a supportive work environment. Encourage team-building activities to strengthen relationships and create a sense of unity.

By supporting the remaining team members through effective communication, validation of emotions, maintaining morale, and monitoring team dynamics, you can ensure a smooth transition after firing an employee. Such compassion and respect will not only preserve the well-being of your team but also enhance their loyalty and productivity, ultimately benefiting the organization as a whole.

Chapter 8 - Learning and Growing from the Experience

Conducting Post-Termination Evaluations and Reflections

Once you have made the difficult decision to terminate an employee, it is important to ensure that the process does not end abruptly. Conducting post-termination evaluations and reflections can provide valuable insights and help create a more compassionate and respectful approach to firing employees.

Post-termination evaluations serve multiple purposes. They allow you to review the termination process and identify any areas for improvement. By reflecting on the entire employee lifecycle, from recruitment to termination, you can identify patterns or issues that might have contributed to the termination. This evaluation can help you refine your hiring and onboarding processes to avoid similar situations in the future.

Additionally, post-termination evaluations give you an opportunity to assess the impact of the termination on the remaining employees and team dynamics. It is crucial to gauge how this event has affected morale and productivity, and to address any concerns or questions that the team may have. By openly discussing the termination and its implications, you can help the team move forward and rebuild trust.

During these evaluations, it is essential to create a safe and non-judgmental environment. Encourage open and honest feedback from both the terminated employee and the remaining team members. Listen attentively and empathetically to their perspectives, allowing them to express their emotions and concerns freely. This approach will foster a sense of psychological safety and encourage employees to share their thoughts and suggestions for improvement.

In addition to evaluations, reflection is a critical component of firing with compassion and respect. Take the time to reflect on the termination process, your own emotions, and the impact it had on others. Consider how you can improve your communication, decision-making, and the overall termination experience.

Reflecting on the termination can also help you identify any personal biases or prejudices that might have influenced your decision-making process. Addressing these biases is essential for creating a fair and inclusive work environment.

By conducting post-termination evaluations and engaging in reflective practices, managers, business owners, and HR professionals can continuously improve their approach to firing employees. This will result in a more compassionate and respectful termination process, benefiting both the terminated employee and the organization as a whole. Remember, it is not just about how you let someone go; it is about how you support them throughout the entire employee journey.

Implementing Improvements in Termination Processes

In today's fast-paced business world, the process of terminating an employee can be a challenging and emotionally charged task for any manager, business owner, or human resource professional. However, it is crucial to approach this delicate matter with compassion and respect, ensuring a graceful goodbye for both parties involved. This subchapter of "The Graceful Goodbye - Firing with Compassion and Respect" aims to provide valuable insights and practical strategies for implementing improvements in termination processes.

1. Developing a compassionate mindset - The first step towards implementing improvements in termination processes is cultivating a compassionate mindset. Managers, business owners, and HR professionals must recognize that employees are individuals with emotions, aspirations, and families to support. By understanding the impact of termination on their lives, it becomes easier to approach the process with empathy and respect.

2. Clear policies and procedures - Implementing improvements in termination processes requires well-defined policies and procedures. Organizations should establish a comprehensive termination policy that outlines the grounds for termination, the steps involved, and the communication process. By having clear guidelines in place, managers can ensure consistency and fairness throughout the process.

3. Effective communication - Communicating the termination decision is a critical aspect of the process. It is essential to deliver the news in a private and respectful setting, allowing the employee to express their thoughts and emotions. Managers should provide honest feedback, focusing on specific performance issues rather than personal attacks. Maintaining a calm and empathetic tone can help ease tension and foster a sense of understanding.

4. Offering support - Termination can be an overwhelming experience for employees. As part of implementing improvements in termination processes, it is crucial to offer support and resources to help the employee transition smoothly. This may include providing information on outplacement services, offering career counseling, or assisting with job search efforts. By extending a helping hand, organizations can demonstrate their commitment to their employees' well-being even during challenging times.

5. Learning from the experience - After each termination, it is vital for managers, business owners, and HR professionals to reflect on the process and identify areas for improvement. Encouraging feedback from all parties involved can lead to valuable insights and help refine termination processes further. By continuously learning and adapting, organizations can create a culture of compassion and respect when it comes to letting employees go.

In conclusion, implementing improvements in termination processes requires a compassionate mindset, clear policies and procedures, effective communication, support, and a commitment to learning and growth. By following these guidelines, managers, business owners, and HR professionals can navigate the challenging task of firing an employee with compassion and respect, ultimately fostering a more harmonious and productive work environment.

Continuously Developing Compassionate Leadership Skills

Subchapter - Continuously Developing Compassionate Leadership Skills

Introduction -

In the fast-paced and competitive business world, the ability to lead with compassion and respect is a crucial skill for managers, business owners, and human resource professionals. This subchapter explores the importance of continuously developing compassionate leadership skills, particularly in the context of firing an employee with compassion and respect. By understanding and implementing these skills, you can create a positive work environment, foster employee growth, and maintain strong relationships within your organization.

1. The Value of Compassionate Leadership -

Compassionate leadership goes beyond simply achieving business goals; it involves understanding and empathizing with employees' needs and concerns. By embracing compassionate leadership, managers can build trust, inspire loyalty, and encourage open communication within their teams. This subchapter explores the various benefits of compassionate leadership and its impact on employee engagement, productivity, and overall organizational success.

2. Developing Empathy and Active Listening Skills -

To become a compassionate leader, it is essential to develop empathy and active listening skills. This section provides practical tips and techniques to enhance your ability to understand and connect with employees on a deeper level. By listening attentively and acknowledging their emotions, you can create a safe and supportive space for employees, even during challenging situations like firing.

3. Emotional Intelligence and Self-Awareness -

Emotional intelligence and self-awareness are critical components of compassionate leadership. This subchapter delves into the importance of understanding your own emotions and effectively managing them to establish a positive work culture. By cultivating emotional intelligence and self-awareness, you can navigate difficult conversations and make decisions with empathy and respect.

4. Providing Constructive Feedback -

Delivering feedback is an integral part of managing employee performance. However, it is crucial to provide feedback in a compassionate and respectful manner. This section offers guidance on giving constructive feedback that focuses on growth and improvement rather than blame or criticism. By adopting this approach, you can help employees understand their areas for development while preserving their dignity and self-esteem.

5. Continuous Learning and Improvement -

Compassionate leadership is an ongoing journey that requires continuous learning and improvement. This subchapter emphasizes the importance of self-reflection, seeking feedback, and engaging in professional development. By investing in your own growth and learning, you can become a better leader and inspire others to follow your compassionate example.

Continuously developing compassionate leadership skills is not only crucial for managing and firing employees compassionately and respectfully but also for creating a positive and thriving work environment. By embracing empathy, active listening, emotional intelligence, and continuous learning, managers, business owners, and human resource professionals can lead with compassion, inspire their teams, and foster an atmosphere of respect and understanding. The next chapter will provide practical strategies and techniques for firing an employee with compassion and respect, building upon the foundation of compassionate leadership developed in this subchapter.

Chapter 9 - Case Studies - Real-Life Examples of Graceful Goodbyes

Case Study 1 - Navigating a Performance-Based Termination

In this case study, we delve into a real-life scenario that illustrates the importance of firing an employee with compassion and respect. The story revolves around a manager named Sarah, who found herself in a challenging situation with one of her team members, John.

John had been with the company for several years and had initially exhibited promise and dedication. However, over time, his performance began to decline, and he consistently missed deadlines and failed to meet quality standards. Sarah, as his manager, had tried various methods to address the issue, including providing additional training, setting clear expectations, and offering guidance and support. Despite her efforts, John's performance did not improve.

Recognizing that terminating an employee is a serious matter, Sarah approached the situation with empathy and compassion. She understood that John's poor performance was not necessarily indicative of his personal character but rather a mismatch between his skills and the requirements of the role. Moreover, Sarah considered the impact of the termination on John's livelihood and self-esteem, as well as the effect on the morale of the remaining team members.

Sarah began by scheduling a private meeting with John to discuss his performance concerns. During this meeting, she highlighted specific examples of his subpar work and addressed the impact it had on the team and the company's overall goals. She allowed John to share his perspective and provided him with an opportunity to express any challenges or concerns he might be facing.

Recognizing the need for fairness and due process, Sarah worked with Human Resources to ensure that all legal and company policy requirements were met. She documented all instances of poor performance, the steps taken to address the issue, and the feedback given to John throughout the process.

To ease the transition for John and demonstrate compassion, Sarah also worked closely with Human Resources to provide him with resources and support for finding alternative employment opportunities. She offered to write a positive reference letter and connected him with networking opportunities within the industry.

Throughout the entire process, Sarah maintained open and honest communication with John, treating him with respect and dignity. She emphasized that the termination was not a personal attack but rather a decision based on business needs and the best interest of the entire team.

This case study serves as a valuable lesson for managers, business owners, and human resource professionals on how to navigate a performance-based termination with compassion and respect. It reinforces the importance of clear communication, fairness, empathy, and support during such difficult situations. By following these principles, organizations can ensure a graceful and respectful goodbye for both the departing employee and the remaining team members.

Case Study 2 - Handling a Downsizing or Restructuring Situation

Introduction -
In today's rapidly changing business environment, downsizing or restructuring is sometimes necessary to ensure the long-term success and sustainability of an organization. However, the process of letting go of employees during such situations can be emotionally challenging for both the management and the employees involved. This case study explores a real-life downsizing scenario and provides insights on how to handle it with compassion and respect.

The Scenario -

In a mid-sized company, the management team decided to restructure certain departments to improve efficiency and reduce costs. As part of this restructuring, several positions were deemed redundant, resulting in the need to let go of a significant number of employees. The management team recognized the importance of handling the downsizing process with compassion and respect, aiming to minimize the adverse impact on both the affected employees and the morale of the remaining workforce.

Key Steps to Handle the Downsizing Situation -

1. Planning and Preparation -
The management team created a detailed downsizing plan that included the identification of affected positions, the criteria for selection, and a timeline for implementation. They also designated a team of HR professionals to oversee the process and ensure fairness and consistency throughout.

2. Open and Transparent Communication -
Recognizing the importance of clear communication, the management team conducted an all-hands meeting to explain the reasons behind the restructuring and the impact it would have on the workforce. They empathetically shared the challenges faced by the organization and their commitment to treating affected employees with compassion and respect.

3. Individual Consultation -
To ensure fairness, HR professionals conducted one-on-one meetings with each affected employee. These consultations provided an opportunity for employees to ask questions, express concerns, and explore potential alternatives or support mechanisms, such as outplacement services, severance packages, or assistance in finding new job opportunities.

4. Support and Transition Assistance -

The management team arranged for counseling sessions and workshops to help affected employees cope with the emotional aspects of job loss and provide guidance on job search strategies. They also facilitated networking opportunities and encouraged employees to leverage their existing skills and experiences.

5. Maintaining Morale and Productivity -

To prevent a decline in morale among the remaining employees, the management team implemented a communication strategy focused on transparency, acknowledging their concerns, and providing reassurance about the organization's future. They also recognized and rewarded the dedication and performance of the retained employees, fostering a positive work environment.

Handling a downsizing or restructuring situation with compassion and respect is crucial for maintaining the trust and loyalty of the workforce. By following a well-planned process, involving open communication, individual consultations, and providing support during the transition, managers, business owners, and HR professionals can ensure that both the affected employees and the organization can navigate this challenging phase with dignity and grace.

Case Study 3 - Termination Due to Misconduct or Policy Violations

Introduction -
In this chapter, we will delve into a real-life case study that highlights the importance of terminating an employee due to misconduct or policy violations with compassion and respect. This case study aims to provide valuable insights and guidance for managers, business owners, and human resource professionals on handling such delicate situations.

Case Study -

Company XYZ, a thriving tech startup, faced a challenging situation when an employee, John, repeatedly violated the company's code of conduct. John's misconduct included insubordination, chronic tardiness, and inappropriate behavior towards colleagues. Despite several warnings and counseling sessions, John failed to rectify his behavior, necessitating termination.

Approach -

Recognizing the significance of firing an employee with compassion and respect, Company XYZ's management team carefully planned the termination process. They understood that while John's actions warranted termination, it was essential to handle the situation with empathy and fairness.

Communication -

The first step was to communicate transparently with John. The company's HR representative, Anna, scheduled a private meeting with John to discuss his ongoing misconduct issues. During this meeting, Anna reiterated the company's expectations and highlighted specific incidents that led to the decision. She also emphasized the impact of John's behavior on the team and the organization as a whole.

Supportive Measures -

Company XYZ understood that termination could be emotionally challenging for John. To soften the blow, the management team offered him a severance package that included a reasonable financial settlement, continued healthcare benefits, and assistance with job placement. These measures aimed to provide a cushion during the transition and demonstrated the company's commitment to treating employees with dignity, even during difficult circumstances.

Outplacement Services -
Recognizing the importance of helping John find new employment, Company XYZ offered him access to outplacement services. These services provided career counseling, resume writing assistance, and interview coaching to support John's job search. By doing so, the company demonstrated their commitment to John's future success, even after termination.

Post-termination Support -
Company XYZ also made efforts to support the remaining team members affected by John's behavior. They organized team-building activities and provided counseling sessions to address any lingering concerns or anxieties. This proactive approach helped maintain a positive work environment and restore employees' confidence.

Takeaway -
This case study highlights the significance of handling terminations due to misconduct or policy violations with compassion and respect. By communicating transparently, providing supportive measures, and offering post-termination support, Company XYZ demonstrated their commitment to both the individual being terminated and the remaining team members. This approach not only mitigated potential legal risks but also fostered a culture of empathy and respect within the organization.

Terminating an employee due to misconduct or policy violations is a challenging and sensitive task. However, by following the principles of compassion and respect, managers, business owners, and human resource professionals can navigate such situations with grace. The case study of Company XYZ serves as a valuable lesson in handling terminations in a humane and empathetic manner.

Case Study 4 - Preventing Violence During Terminations

Introduction -

As managers, business owners, and human resource professionals, one of the most challenging aspects of our roles can be terminating an employee. It is a delicate process that requires empathy, compassion, and respect. However, in some cases, terminations can lead to volatile situations, putting both the employee and the organization at risk. In this case study, we will explore effective strategies for preventing violence during terminations and maintaining a safe and respectful work environment.

Understanding the Potential for Violence -

Terminations can trigger a range of emotions in employees, including anger, frustration, and a sense of betrayal. While the majority of terminations occur without incident, it is crucial to recognize the potential for violence and take proactive measures to prevent it. By understanding the warning signs and implementing preventive measures, managers can minimize the risk of violence during terminations.

Identifying Warning Signs -

There are several warning signs that an employee may exhibit before or during a termination that could indicate a potential for violence. These signs include excessive anger or hostility, threats made towards colleagues or the organization, a history of aggression, or sudden changes in behavior. It is essential to train managers and human resource professionals to recognize these signs and take appropriate action.

Creating a Safe Environment -

To prevent violence during terminations, it is crucial to create a safe environment for all parties involved. This includes conducting terminations in a private and secure location, having a security professional present when necessary, and establishing clear protocols for handling difficult terminations. By ensuring the physical safety of everyone involved, the potential for violence can be significantly reduced.

Effective Communication and Active Listening -
During terminations, effective communication and active listening skills are paramount. Managers and human resource professionals must approach the process with empathy and compassion, allowing the employee to express their emotions and concerns. By actively listening and acknowledging their feelings, it becomes less likely for the situation to escalate into violence.

Offering Support and Resources -
To prevent violence and foster a compassionate environment, it is essential to offer support and resources to employees who are being terminated. Providing information on outplacement services, career counseling, or access to employee assistance programs can help ease the transition and reduce feelings of anger or despair.

Conclusion -
Terminating an employee is never an easy task, but by approaching it with compassion and respect, the risk of violence can be minimized. By recognizing the warning signs, creating a safe environment, practicing effective communication, and offering support, managers, business owners, and human resource professionals can navigate terminations with grace and ensure the well-being of all involved parties. Remember, a graceful goodbye is not only a reflection of the organization's values but also an opportunity for personal growth and development for the terminated employee.

Chapter 10 - Building a Compassionate and Respectful Workplace Culture

Establishing Clear Values and Expectations During Onboarding

One of the most critical aspects of onboarding new employees is establishing clear values and expectations right from the start.

This is especially important when it comes to building a compassionate and respectful culture within an organization. In this subchapter, we will explore the significance of establishing clear values and expectations during the onboarding process and how it contributes to firing an employee with compassion and respect.

Managers, business owners, and human resource professionals play a vital role in shaping the organizational culture. By clearly communicating the values and expectations during the onboarding process, they set the foundation for employees' behavior and performance. This is particularly essential when it comes to the delicate task of firing an employee. When values and expectations are clearly defined, employees are more likely to understand the consequences of their actions and make informed decisions that align with the organization's values.

During the onboarding process, it is crucial to communicate the organization's core values, code of conduct, and expectations for performance and behavior. This can be done through orientation sessions, employee handbooks, and one-on-one conversations. By emphasizing the importance of compassion and respect in the workplace, managers can create an environment where employees feel valued, supported, and motivated to perform at their best.

When an employee needs to be fired, it is essential to handle the situation with compassion and respect. By establishing clear values and expectations from the beginning, managers can refer back to those principles when addressing performance or behavior issues. This allows the conversation to focus on the disconnect between the employee's actions and the organization's values, rather than personal attacks or blame.

Furthermore, by consistently upholding these values and expectations throughout the employee's tenure, managers can ensure fairness and consistency in the firing process. This helps to minimize the emotional impact on both the employee being fired and the remaining employees, as they understand that everyone is held to the same standards.

In conclusion, establishing clear values and expectations during the onboarding process is crucial for creating a compassionate and respectful culture within an organization. By effectively communicating these values, managers, business owners, and human resource professionals can lay the foundation for firing an employee with compassion and respect. This subchapter provides valuable insights and practical strategies for setting clear expectations during onboarding to ensure a graceful and respectful goodbye when necessary.

Training Managers and Leaders in Compassionate Leadership

In today's fast-paced business world, it is essential for managers and leaders to possess not only technical skills but also the ability to lead with compassion and empathy. Gone are the days when a leader's success was solely measured by the bottom line; now, organizations are recognizing the importance of valuing their employees and treating them with dignity, even during challenging times such as firing an employee. This subchapter aims to provide managers, business owners, and human resource professionals with the tools and knowledge to become compassionate leaders in the context of terminating an employee.

Compassionate leadership is about understanding the human element in every interaction and decision. It is about recognizing that employees are not just assets or resources but individuals with their own hopes, dreams, and challenges. When it comes to firing an employee, compassion and respect are paramount. This subchapter will explore various strategies and techniques that can be employed to ensure that the termination process is handled with sensitivity and empathy.

First and foremost, it is crucial to establish a culture of compassion within the organization. This can be achieved through comprehensive training programs that emphasize the importance of empathy and understanding in all aspects of leadership. By providing managers and leaders with the necessary knowledge and skills, organizations can foster an environment where compassion is valued and practiced.

Secondly, this subchapter will delve into specific techniques for conducting termination meetings with compassion and respect. It will outline strategies for preparing for the meeting, delivering the news in a sensitive manner, and providing support to the employee during and after the termination. By following these guidelines, managers and leaders can ensure that the employee's dignity is maintained and that they are treated with the respect they deserve.

Furthermore, this subchapter will address the emotional impact that firing an employee can have on managers and leaders. It will explore methods to manage and cope with the emotional toll of such difficult decisions while still adhering to compassionate leadership principles.

Overall, this subchapter serves as a guide for managers, business owners, and human resource professionals to develop their skills in compassionate leadership during the challenging task of terminating an employee. By embracing empathy, understanding, and respect, leaders can navigate these difficult situations with grace and ensure that the dignity of all individuals involved is upheld.

Promoting Open Communication and Conflict Resolution Skills

In today's fast-paced business world, effective communication and conflict resolution skills are essential for managers, business owners, and human resource professionals. These skills not only contribute to a harmonious work environment but also play a crucial role when it comes to terminating an employee with compassion and respect. In this subchapter, we will explore the importance of open communication and conflict resolution, and how they can be utilized during the challenging process of firing an employee.

Open communication is the foundation of any successful organization. By fostering an environment where employees feel encouraged to express their thoughts, concerns, and opinions, managers can build trust and establish strong relationships within the workplace. When it comes to firing an employee, open communication becomes even more critical. It allows managers to provide honest feedback, discuss performance issues, and address any concerns before making the difficult decision to terminate.

Conflict resolution skills are equally vital in the firing process. Often, terminating an employee can lead to heightened emotions, tension, and even potential conflicts. By honing conflict resolution skills, managers can navigate these challenging situations with empathy and professionalism. Effective conflict resolution techniques, such as active listening, empathy, and finding common ground, can help diffuse tense situations and ensure a respectful and compassionate termination process.

Promoting open communication and conflict resolution skills also extends beyond the termination itself. By fostering a culture of open communication and providing conflict resolution training, managers can create a more inclusive and supportive work environment. This, in turn, can reduce the likelihood of future terminations and enhance overall employee satisfaction and retention rates.

In conclusion, promoting open communication and conflict resolution skills is crucial for managers, business owners, and human resource professionals. These skills not only contribute to a positive work environment but also play a pivotal role in handling the challenging task of terminating an employee with compassion and respect. By investing in open communication and conflict resolution training, businesses can create a workplace culture that values transparent communication, empathy, and respectful conflict resolution – resulting in better employee relations, increased productivity, and ultimately, a graceful goodbye when necessary.

Addressing Issues Early with Empathy

In the fast-paced world of business, managers and business owners often find themselves facing the difficult task of having to fire an employee. However, it is crucial to approach this process with compassion and respect, ensuring that the employee's dignity is maintained throughout. In this subchapter, we will explore the importance of addressing issues early on and how empathy can play a significant role in the graceful goodbye process.

As managers, it is essential to address issues as soon as they arise. By promptly identifying and addressing problems, you can prevent them from escalating and potentially leading to termination. This proactive approach allows you to give employees an opportunity to rectify their mistakes, grow professionally, and contribute positively to the organization. By addressing issues early, you not only foster a culture of open communication but also demonstrate your commitment to the well-being of your employees.

Empathy is a crucial element when addressing issues with employees. By putting yourself in their shoes, you can better understand their perspective, motivations, and challenges. This understanding allows you to approach the conversation with empathy, respect, and genuine concern for the individual's welfare. By showing empathy, you can create an environment where employees feel heard, valued, and supported, even in difficult times.

When addressing issues early with empathy, it is important to approach conversations with a non-judgmental attitude. Instead of focusing solely on the problem at hand, take the time to understand the underlying causes and work collaboratively towards finding a solution. This approach encourages employees to take ownership of their actions, fostering personal growth and development.

Furthermore, addressing issues early with empathy allows for the possibility of course correction. This means providing employees with the necessary tools, guidance, and support to improve their performance or behavior. By offering constructive feedback and coaching, you can help employees overcome challenges and enhance their skills, ensuring that termination is a last resort.

In conclusion, addressing issues early with empathy is a fundamental aspect of firing an employee with compassion and respect. By promptly addressing problems, showing empathy, and providing the necessary support, managers and business owners can foster a positive work environment that values both the individual and the organization. Remember, a graceful goodbye is not just about the end result but also about the journey taken to reach that point.

Chapter 11 - Conclusion - Embracing the Graceful Goodbye

Reflecting on the Impact of Compassionate Terminations

In today's fast-paced and competitive business environment, managers, business owners, and human resource professionals often find themselves facing the difficult task of terminating an employee. The process of firing an employee is undoubtedly one of the most challenging aspects of leadership. It is a decision that affects not only the individual being let go but also the entire team and the organization as a whole.

In the subchapter titled "Reflecting on the Impact of Compassionate Terminations," we delve into the profound effects that firing an employee with compassion and respect can have on both the departing individual and the remaining team members. This subchapter aims to provide valuable insights and guidance to managers, business owners, and HR professionals on how to navigate this process with empathy and grace.

The traditional approach to termination often involves cold, impersonal methods that focus solely on the bottom line. However, the times are changing, and a new paradigm is emerging – one that acknowledges the importance of compassion and respect in the workplace. By adopting compassionate terminations, leaders can not only protect the dignity and emotional well-being of the employee being let go but also maintain the morale and productivity of the remaining team.

We explore the tangible benefits that compassionate terminations bring to the organization. By conducting the process with empathy, managers can preserve the departing employee's self-esteem and help them transition to new opportunities more smoothly. This, in turn, contributes to a positive employer brand, attracting and retaining top talent in the long run.

Moreover, we discuss the impact of compassionate terminations on the remaining team members. When handled poorly, terminations can create fear, uncertainty, and dissatisfaction among the remaining employees. However, by approaching the process with compassion and respect, leaders can inspire trust and foster a sense of loyalty among the team. This subchapter provides practical strategies to mitigate the negative impacts of terminations on team dynamics and maintain productivity during times of change.

"The Graceful Goodbye - Firing with Compassion and Respect" is a valuable resource for managers, business owners, and HR professionals seeking guidance on how to fire an employee with compassion and respect. By reflecting on the impact of compassionate terminations, readers will gain a deeper understanding of the positive outcomes that arise from treating departing employees with dignity and empathy. Through real-life examples and practical advice, this subchapter equips leaders with the tools necessary to navigate the challenging process of termination while fostering a culture of compassion and respect in their organizations.

Committing to a Culture of Compassion and Respect

In today's fast-paced and competitive business world, the task of firing an employee can be a daunting and sensitive challenge for any manager, business owner, or human resource professional. However, it is crucial to approach this difficult task with compassion and respect to ensure a graceful goodbye and maintain a positive work environment.

Creating a culture of compassion and respect within your organization should be a core value embraced by every member of your team. By committing to this culture, you can foster an atmosphere of empathy, understanding, and fairness, even in the face of difficult decisions such as terminating an employee's contract.

One crucial aspect of firing an employee with compassion and respect is effective communication. Open and honest dialogue should be maintained throughout the entire process. Clearly explain the reasons for the termination and provide the employee with constructive feedback on areas for improvement. Remember, the goal is not to belittle or humiliate the individual but to help them grow and find better opportunities elsewhere.

Another important element is offering support to the employee during this transitional period. Consider providing resources such as career counseling, resume writing assistance, or job search workshops. By showing genuine care for the employee's well-being and future prospects, you can soften the blow and help them navigate their next steps.

Furthermore, it is essential to handle the termination in a private and confidential manner. Respect the employee's privacy by conducting the conversation in a discreet location, away from prying eyes. This will allow them to process their emotions without unnecessary scrutiny or embarrassment.

To truly commit to a culture of compassion and respect, it is also crucial to learn from each termination experience. Conduct exit interviews to gain valuable insights into the reasons behind the termination and identify any potential systemic issues within your organization. By continuously improving your processes and policies, you can minimize the need for future terminations and create a more supportive work environment.

In conclusion, firing an employee with compassion and respect is a challenging task, but it is essential for maintaining a positive work environment and preserving your organization's reputation. By committing to a culture of compassion and respect, practicing effective communication, providing support during the transition, maintaining privacy, and learning from each experience, you can ensure a graceful goodbye and lay the foundation for a more compassionate and respectful workplace.

Inspiring Others to Embrace the Graceful Goodbye

In today's rapidly changing business landscape, managers, business owners, and human resource professionals face numerous challenges, one of the most difficult being the task of letting an employee go. When faced with the daunting responsibility of terminating someone's employment, it is crucial to do so with compassion and respect. This subchapter, titled "Inspiring Others to Embrace the Graceful Goodbye," from the book "The Graceful Goodbye - Firing with Compassion and Respect," aims to guide managers, business owners, and HR professionals on how to navigate this delicate situation.

The graceful goodbye is not just about the act of letting someone go; it is about creating a culture of empathy and understanding within an organization. By fostering an environment where employees are treated with compassion and respect, even during difficult times, organizations can build strong relationships built on trust and loyalty.

To inspire others to embrace the graceful goodbye, it is essential to lead by example. Managers must demonstrate empathy and understanding throughout the entire process. By approaching the situation with kindness and sensitivity, managers can help the employee understand the reasons behind the decision and support them during the transition period.

Furthermore, effective communication plays a vital role in the graceful goodbye. Managers should be transparent about the decision-making process, ensuring that employees understand the rationale behind their termination. This transparency helps to alleviate any feelings of confusion or injustice and allows the employee to gain closure.

In addition, providing resources and support during the transition period is crucial. Managers should offer guidance on how to update resumes, practice interview skills, and seek new job opportunities. By offering assistance, managers can empower employees to bounce back, fostering their personal growth and professional development.

The graceful goodbye is not just about the employee being let go; it is also about the impact on those who stay. Managers should address any concerns or anxieties that may arise among the remaining employees. Holding open discussions and providing reassurance can help maintain a positive work environment, preventing any negative impacts on productivity or morale.

By inspiring others to embrace the graceful goodbye, managers, business owners, and HR professionals can transform the termination process from a stressful event into an opportunity for growth and development. By treating employees with compassion and respect, organizations can build a reputation as an employer that values its workforce, leading to increased loyalty and improved employee morale.